To:

From:

Incredible Candy

for your sweet tooth

Printed in the United States of America

ISBN 1-56383-044-2

TABLE OF CONTENTS

CANDY HINTS

HINTS

Never double a recipe. If a large amount of candy is desired, make another batch.

Humidity and altitude affect candy. If it is rainy, cook candy to a degree or so higher than the recipe indicates. Consult an altitude table to determine the boiling point in your area. You may want to test the temperature of boiling water before you make candy. If the water boils at $210°$ instead of the normal of $212°$, for example, subtract $2°$ from the temperature specified in the recipe.

Never let water get into your chocolate or it will be ruined.

COLD WATER TEST: Remove pan from heat. Add a few drops of syrup into a bowl of very cold (not ice) water. Form drops into balls - its firmness indicates temperature of syrup:

Thread	230 - 234°
Soft Ball	234 - 238°
Medium Ball	238 - 244°
Firm Ball	244 - 248°
Very Hard Ball	254 - 265°
Light Crack	265 - 285°
Hard Crack	290 - 300°

THERMOMETER TEST: Clip candy thermometer to pan after syrup boils (bulb must be covered with boiling liquid, not just foam). Read thermometer with eyes level with fluid in indication column, while syrup is boiling. Check thermometer in boiling water. If it registers above or below 212°, add or subtract degrees to make same allowance in recipe.

FUDGE REPAIR

TO SOFTEN: If fudge is smooth, but became too stiff before you poured it out, knead with your hands until it softens; press into buttered pan or shape in roll and slice.

TO FIRM UP: If fudge doesn't set, it was poured too soon or not cooked enough. To remedy, add ¼ cup milk, stir, recook and beat.

FUDGE TIPS

- Prevent crystals from very start by buttering sides of saucepan.

- Choose a heavy, high-sided pan that's smooth inside.

- Stir fudge until it comes to boiling and <u>all</u> grains of sugar have dissolved.

- When syrup boils, clip on candy thermometer. Once it reaches 220°, <u>check often</u>, cook to soft ball stage (234°).

- Cool to 110° before beating. Don't ever stir in butter - just put on top. Set pan in sink of cold water (no ice!).

- When 110°, rest pan on potholder; beat vigorously with wooden spoon. <u>Do not rest or stop too soon.</u>

- When fudge stiffens and loses gloss, add nuts and push from pan with rubber spatula - don't scrape sides. Score while warm.

4

CHOCOLATE & FUDGE CANDY

CHOCOLATE TIPS

• Chocolate-dipping should not be attempted on hot or damp days. Best results are obtained if room is fairly cool, about 65°.

• Caramels, nutmeats, candied fruits, stuffed dried fruits or molded fondant centers may be chocolate-dipped. Mold fondant centers a day or two before dipping, otherwise fondant leaks through chocolate coating.

• Use at least 1 pound dipping chocolate; smaller amounts are more difficult to handle. Finely shave chocolate with knife or vegetable shredder. Have water in bottom of double boiler hot, but not boiling (115 to 120°); there should be enough water to touch the top vessel. Place chocolate over hot water and stir constantly until melted and free from lumps. Remove from

(continued)

5

water and stir until thick and cool (82 to 86°). Again, place over the hot water, cooled to 86 to 88°. Working rapidly, drop one center at a time into chocolate; press under chocolate with spoon so it is entirely covered. Lift out with fork; scrape excess chocolate from fork and place center on tray covered with waxed paper. Scrape any hardened chocolate from fork into another vessel, not into double boiler.

• Never allow water to come in contact with dipping chocolate; it causes gray streaks. If chocolate becomes too stiff to use, heat as at first.

• Grated cocoa butter may be added to dipping chocolate to give it body and keep it smooth.

CHOCOLATE DIPS

1 stick margarine, melted
2 C. super chunk peanut
   butter

1 lb. bag powdered sugar
3 C. crispy rice
2 C. chocolate chips
¼ bar paraffin wax

Mix margarine, peanut butter, powdered sugar, and crispy rice together well. Press or shape into round balls. Melt chocolate chips and paraffin wax in double boiler. Do not let the water boil. Dip each ball in melted chocolate. Place on wax paper on a tray in refrigerator to harden. May be kept in the refrigerator or stored in freezer.

COCOA FUDGE

⅔ C. cocoa
3 C. sugar
⅛ tsp. salt

1½ C. heavy cream or
   non-dairy liquid cream
   substitute
¼ C. butter
1 tsp. vanilla

Combine cocoa, sugar, salt and heavy cream in a large saucepan. Bring to a rolling boil, then reduce heat to medium and cook to 234° <u>without stirring.</u> Remove from the heat and add butter and vanilla. Do not stir. Cool to lukewarm (about 110°). Beat by hand or with mixer until fudge thickens and loses some of its gloss. Quickly spread fudge in a lightly buttered 8" square pan. When cool, cut into squares. Makes about 49 pieces.

MELLOW FUDGE

3 C. sugar
3 rounded T. cocoa
1 scant C. milk
5 T. white syrup

Pinch of salt
1 tsp. vanilla
1 T. butter
1 C. nuts

Mix sugar, cocoa, milk, syrup, and salt and boil to soft ball stage. Then add vanilla, butter and nuts and let stand 10 minutes. Now beat until mixture is creamy. Then spread into buttered pan. Cut when cold.

PEANUT BUTTER FUDGE

2 C. sugar
½ C. evaporated milk
2 T. water

⅓ C. peanut butter
1 tsp. vanilla
1 T. butter

Mix in saucepan the sugar, milk and water. Cook slowly, stirring occasionally to 236° on a candy thermometer or until a few drops form a soft ball when dropped into water. Remove from heat. Cool at room temperature without stirring until lukewarm or until hand can be held comfortable on bottom of pan. Add peanut butter, vanilla and butter. Beat until smooth. Pour into greased pan and cut into squares when cool. Makes 3 dozen pieces.

NO FAIL FUDGE

3 C. sugar
¾ C. butter or margarine
1-5 oz. can evaporated milk
1-12 oz. pkg. _real_ chocolate
 chips

1-10 oz. jar marshmallow
 creme
1 C. chopped nuts
1 tsp. vanilla

Combine sugar, butter and milk in buttered, large glass mixing bowl; cover.
Microwave on _defrost_ for 15 minutes. Stir and microwave for 8 to 10 minutes
or until mixture forms a soft ball in cold water. Stir in chocolate chips until
melted. Fold in marshmallow creme, nuts and vanilla. Pour in buttered
9x13" pan. Chill until firm.

MAMIE EISENHOWER'S FUDGE

4½ C. sugar
Pinch of salt

4 T. butter
1 can evaporated milk

Boil the above ingredients for 6 minutes (time starts after it comes to a boil). Remove from heat and add:

12 oz. semi-sweet chocolate
12 oz. German sweet
  chocolate

1 pt. marshmallow creme
2 C. nutmeats

Beat until everything is melted. Pour out onto waxed paper or buttered cookie sheet.

FUDGE DELUXE

2 C. sugar
½ C. cream
½ C. milk
3 T. butter

½ C. syrup
1½ tsp. vanilla
1 square chocolate
½ C. chopped nuts

Combine sugar, cream, milk, butter and syrup in saucepan over low heat, stirring only to keep from burning. Cook to soft ball stage (235°). Add vanilla. Pour half of mixture into bowl and beat right away until creamy. Then pour into buttered pan. Put the chocolate and nuts into other half. Beat until creamy and pour over white layer. Cool; cut in squares.

PANOCHA

1½ C. granulated sugar
1 C. brown sugar
⅓ C. light cream
⅓ C. milk

2 T. butter or margarine
1 tsp. vanilla
½ C. broken walnuts or
   pecans

Butter sides of heavy 2-quart saucepan. In it, combine sugars, cream, milk and butter. Heat over medium heat, stirring constantly, until sugar dissolves and mixture comes to a boil. Cook to soft ball stage (238°), stirring only if necessary. Immediately remove from heat and cool to lukewarm (110°) without stirring. Add vanilla. Beat vigorously until fudge becomes very thick and starts to lose its gloss. Quickly stir in nuts and spread in buttered, shallow pan. Score while warm. Top each square with nut half.

ORANGE CARAMEL FUDGE

3 C. sugar
½ C. hot water
1 C. evaporated milk
¼ tsp. salt

4 T. butter or margarine
2 tsp. grated orange rind
1 C. chopped nuts

Put 1 cup sugar in heavy saucepan. Cook and stir over medium heat until sugar is melted and golden colored. Add water and stir until sugar is dissolved. Stir in remaining sugar, milk and salt. Cook over low heat, stirring occasionally, until mixture reaches 242° on a candy thermometer. Remove from heat. Add butter, orange rind and nuts. Beat until thick and creamy. Turn into greased aluminum foil pan. Cool; mark into squares. Makes 1½ pounds.

EASY MINT FUDGE

4 C. sugar
1-14½ oz. can (1¾ C.)
  evaporated milk
½ C. butter or margarine

1-12 oz. pkg. chocolate mint
  wafers
½ lb. marshmallows
  (about 32)
California walnut halves

Combine sugar, milk and butter. Cook to soft ball stage (234 to 236°), stirring constantly. Remove from heat. Add mint wafers and marshmallows. Stir until blended. Pour immediately in buttered 13x9x2" pan. Cut in squares. Place walnut half on each piece.

EASY FUDGE

½ C. cocoa   1 stick butter
1 lb. (3½ C.) powdered sugar   1 tsp. vanilla
¼ C. milk   ½ C. nuts

Blend cocoa and sugar; add milk and butter, but do not mix. Microwave on high for 2 minutes. Add vanilla and nuts; stir. Pour in greased dish. Place in freezer for 20 minutes or refrigerate 1 hour before serving.

CHOCOLATE FUDGE

2-1 oz. squares unsweetened
  chocolate, grated
⅔ C. milk, scalded
2 C. sugar

1 T. light corn syrup
2 T. butter
1 tsp. vanilla extract

Melt chocolate in scalded milk; stir until blended. Add sugar and corn syrup; cook slowly, stirring until sugar dissolves. Bring to boiling; cover and cook 3 minutes. Uncover and continue cooking to soft ball stage (236 to 238°), stirring frequently. Remove from heat; add butter and cool to lukewarm (110°) without stirring. Add vanilla extract and beat vigorously unit candy is very thick and loses its gloss. Quickly pour into greased pan. When firm, cut in squares. If desired, add 1 cup broken nutmeats shortly before pouring. Fudge may be kneaded when hard, formed into rolls and sliced. Makes 2 dozen pieces.

4½ MINUTE FUDGE

4½ C. sugar
1 large can evaporated milk
3 bars sweet German
  chocolate
2 pkgs. chocolate chips

1 pt. marshmallow creme
½ tsp. salt
1 C. nuts (optional)
1 tsp. vanilla

Boil sugar and evaporated milk exactly 4½ minutes, stirring constantly.
Add all of the other ingredients and stir until melted. Pour into a buttered
pan, 9x13". Makes 5 pounds.

PINEAPPLE FUDGE

2 C. granulated sugar
1 C. brown sugar
½ C. light cream
1-#2 can (2½ C.) crushed
  pineapple, drained

2 T. butter or margarine
2 tsp. ginger
2 tsp. vanilla
1 C. broken California
  walnuts

Combine sugars, cream and pineapple; cook, stirring occasionally, to soft ball stage (236°). Remove from heat; add butter, ginger and vanilla. Cool at room temperature, without stirring, until lukewarm (110°). Beat until mixture loses its gloss; add nuts. Pour into buttered 8x8x2" pan. Score candy into squares; press walnut half on each, if desired. Cut when firm. Makes about 24 pieces.

SOUR CREAM FUDGE

2 C. sugar
½ tsp. salt
1 C. sour cream

2 T. butter or margarine
½ C. broken pecans or other
  nuts

Combine sugar, salt and sour cream. Cook, stirring occasionally, to soft ball stage (236°). Add butter. Cool at room temperature, without stirring, until lukewarm (110°). Beat until mixture loses gloss; add nuts. Spread in buttered 8x8x2" pan. When firm, cut in squares. Makes about 24 pieces.

SNOW-WHITE FUDGE

3 C. sugar	2 tsp. vanilla
1½ C. milk	½ C. chopped dried
¾ tsp. salt	California apricots
3 T. butter or margarine	½ C. marshmallow creme
	⅓ C. chopped walnuts

Butter sides of 3-quart saucepan. Mix sugar, milk and salt in saucepan. Stir and heat until sugar dissolves and mixture boils. Cook, without stirring, to soft ball stage (238°). Stir in butter and vanilla. Place in pan of cold water and cool to lukewarm without stirring. Add apricots and beat until mixture holds shape. Stir in marshmallow creme and walnuts; beat until glossy. Spread fudge in buttered 9" square pan. When fudge sets, cut into 32 bars.

MARBLED PEANUT BUTTER FUDGE

6 C. sugar
1½ C. (3 sticks) margarine
1-12 oz. can evaporated
  milk

1 jar (13 g) marshmallow
  creme
2 tsp. vanilla
1 C. semi-sweet chocolate
1 C. peanut butter

Mix sugar, margarine and milk in heavy saucepan; bring to full rolling boil, stirring constantly. Continue boiling 5 minutes over medium heat or until candy thermometer reaches 234° F., stirring constantly to prevent scorching. Remove from heat. Stir in marshmallow creme and vanilla. Divide mixture into 2 equal portions. Stir chocolate into one portion until melted and blended. Stir peanut butter into other portion until blended. Pour peanut butter mixture into greased 9x13" baking pan. Top with chocolate mixture. Cut through fudge with knife several times to give marble effect. Cool. Cut into squares.

MILLION DOLLAR FUDGE

4½ C. sugar
Pinch of salt
2 T. butter or oleo
1 large can evaporated
milk

12 oz. pkg. semi-sweet
chocolate chips
12 oz. pkg. German sweet
chocolate
2 small jars marshmallow
creme
2 C. nuts

Boil first 4 ingredients for 6 minutes. Combine remaining ingredients in large mixing bowl. Pour syrup over. Beat until chocolate is melted. Pour in 1" deep cookie sheet. Let stand a few hours before cutting. Store in tin.

MARTHA WASHINGTON FUDGE
(NO COOK)

2 lbs. powdered sugar
1 can condensed milk

¼ C. soft butter
2 tsp. vanilla
3 C. chopped nuts
Melted chocolate

Mix all ingredients and chill. Roll into balls. Dip in melted chocolate.

FUDGE DROPS

8 oz. milk chocolate candy bar   1 can evaporated milk
8 oz. marshmallow creme   1 C. chopped pecans
12 oz. chocolate chips

Melt candy bar, marshmallow creme, chocolate chips and evaporated milk together. Remove from heat. Stir in nuts. Drop by teaspoon onto wax paper and let set for 12 hours.

PEANUT BUTTER CUPS

1 C. margarine
1½ C. smooth peanut butter
1½ C. graham cracker
  crumbs

1 box powdered sugar
1-6 oz. pkg. chocolate chips
Roasted peanuts

Melt margarine. Add peanut butter. Add cracker crumbs and sugar and mix well. Put liner in muffin tins. Press mixture into muffin tins. Melt chocolate chips in a double boiler and spread on top. Sprinkle with roasted peanuts. Let set for about 1 hour in a cool place, then serve.

PEANUT BUTTER KISSES

⅓ C. corn syrup
⅓ C. peanut butter
½ C. nonfat dry milk

⅓ C. powdered sugar
Chopped nuts (optional)

In a small mixing bowl, combine corn syrup with peanut butter. When well mixed, gradually add nonfat dry milk and sifted powdered sugar. Shape into a roll about ¾" in diameter; roll in chopped nuts, if desired. Wrap in waxed paper and chill. Cut into 24-1" pieces.

TOOTSIE ROLLS

2 T. butter or margarine
½ C. white syrup
2 squares melted chocolate

1 tsp. vanilla
3 C. powdered sugar
¾ C. dry instant milk

Mix all ingredients together and knead. Roll into ¾" roll. Cut in slices and let stand. Wrap.

CHOCOLATE FLAKE CANDY

1 C. pecan meats
1 C. dates
5 C. cornflakes

¼ tsp. salt
1 lb. sweet milk chocolate
2-1 oz. sqs. unsweetened
    chocolate

Combine chopped pecan meats, dates, cornflakes and salt. Melt sweet milk chocolate and unsweetened chocolate in double boiler; pour over cornflake mixture; mix lightly. Drop from teaspoon onto waxed paper. Chill. Keep in cool place. Makes 4 dozen pieces.

BUTTERSCOTCH RUM FUDGE

1 C. golden raisins, chopped
¼ C. light rum
2 C. firmly packed brown
  sugar
1 C. sugar
½ C. butter or margarine
1 C. evaporated milk
1-7 oz. jar marshmallow
  creme
1-12 oz. pkg. butterscotch
  morsels
½ C. chopped pecans
½ C. chopped walnuts
1 tsp. rum extract
½ tsp. vanilla

Combine raisins and rum in a small bowl; cover and let stand 8 hours.
Combine brown sugar, sugar, margarine and milk in 3-quart saucepan;
cook over medium heat, stirring constantly to soft ball stage (238°). Remove
from heat, stir in marshmallow creme and butterscotch morsels. Add raisin
mixture and remaining ingredients; stir well. Spread mixture into buttered
8" square pan. Cool and cut into squares. Store in airtight container. 31

FRUIT CANDY

STRAWBERRIES SUPREME

2-3 oz. pkgs. strawberry
 jello
1 C. ground pecans
1 C. flaked coconut
¾ C. sweetened condensed
 milk

½ tsp. vanilla
Red sugar
Blanched, sliced almonds

Combine jello, nuts and coconut. Stir in milk and vanilla and mix well. Chill 1 hour. Shape into strawberries and roll in red sugar. Tint almonds in green food coloring and insert in top for leaves. Put in container and let set a week or more.

LEMON FRUIT-JELL CANDY

1-6 oz. bottle liquid fruit
  pectin
2 T. water
½ tsp. baking soda
1 C. sugar

1 C. light corn syrup
2 tsp. lemon extract
10 drops yellow food
  coloring
Granulated sugar

Combine fruit pectin and water in 2-quart saucepan. Stir in baking soda. (Mixture will foam slightly.) Mix sugar and corn syrup in a large saucepan. Place both saucepans over high heat and cook both mixtures, stirring alternately, until foam has thinned from fruit pectin mixture and sugar mixture is boiling rapidly, 3 to 5 minutes. Pour fruit pectin mixture in a slow, steady stream into boiling sugar mixture, stirring constantly. Boil and stir 1 minute longer. Remove from heat. Stir in lemon extract and yellow food coloring. Pour immediately into a buttered 9" square pan. Let stand at room temperature until mixture is cool and firm, about 3 hours. Invert pan onto waxed paper which has been sprinkled with granulated sugar. Cut candy into ¾" squares or shapes and roll in the sugar. Allow candy to stand awhile; roll again in sugar to prevent stickiness. Let stand overnight, uncovered, at room temperature before packing or storing. Makes about 1 pound.

Candies may also be rolled in powdered sugar, colored sprinkles or crystal sugar, or dipped in melted semi-sweet chocolate.

CRANBERRY JELLY CANDY

1-16 oz. can jellied
  cranberry sauce
3-3 oz. pkgs. cherry,
  raspberry or orange
  gelatin
1 C. sugar

½ bottle liquid fruit pectin
  (3 fl. oz.)
1 C. chopped nuts
Additional sugar or flaked
  coconut

Beat cranberry sauce in a saucepan until smooth. Bring to a boil. Stir in gelatin and sugar; simmer 10 minutes, stirring frequently, until gelatin is dissolved. Remove from heat. Stir in fruit pectin; then add nuts and stir 10 minutes to prevent nuts from floating. Pour into buttered 9" square pan. Chill until firm, about 2 hours. Invert onto waxed paper, which has been sprinkled with additional sugar or coconut. Cut candy into ¾" squares with spatula dipped in warm water; roll in sugar. After about an hour, roll in sugar or coconut again to prevent stickiness. Makes about 2 pounds of candy.

CANDIED ORANGE PEEL

7 large oranges
1½ C. water
2 C. sugar
3 T. honey

¼ tsp. salt
1 tsp. unflavored gelatin
Sugar

Cut oranges into fourths. Remove pulp and scrape away white membrane. Cut peel into strips. Place peel in saucepan, cover with water and simmer 15 minutes. Drain. Pour 1½ cups water over peel. Add 2 cups sugar, honey and salt. Cook over low heat for 45 minutes, stirring occasionally. Soften gelatin in ¼ cup water. Remove orange mixture from heat; add softened gelatin. Stir to dissolve. When cool, drain candy; roll in sugar. Let dry overnight on waxed paper. Store in a covered container. Makes about ¾ pound.

UNCOOKED FRUIT CARAMELS

1 C. seeded raisins
½ C. dried apricots
½ C. dried figs
1 C. pitted dates
½ C. candied orange peel

6 candied cherries
1 C. California walnuts
3 T. orange juice
Confectioners' sugar

Wash raisins, apricots, figs. Put first 7 ingredients through food chopper. Add enough orange juice to hold fruit and nuts together; mix well. Press into greased 8x8x2" pan. Chill overnight in refrigerator. Cut in squares. Roll in powdered sugar.

CARAMEL APPLES

1 lb. (56) vanilla caramels
2 T. water
Dash of salt

6 wooden skewers
6 crisp, medium apples
Chopped nuts

Melt caramels with water in double boiler, stirring frequently, until smooth. Add salt. Stick a skewer into bottom end of each apple. Dip apple in caramel syrup and turn until surface is completely covered. (Add a few drops of water if syrup is too stiff.) <u>At once</u>, roll bottom half of coated apple in chopped nuts. Set on cookie sheet covered with waxed paper. Chill until firm.

WONDERFUL CANDY

2-1 lb. boxes powdered
  sugar
12 oz. cream cheese,
  softened

½ C. finely chopped cherries
½ C. finely chopped nuts
Almond or vanilla extract

Sift sugar. Mash cream cheese. Combine all ingredients, using 1 small bottle of extract or as much as desired. Knead as bread. Pack mixture into a square tin and chill in freezer before cutting.

APRICOT CANDY

1-7 oz. jar marshmallow
  creme
1 T. margarine
¼ tsp. vanilla
¼ tsp. grated orange rind

¼ tsp. salt
3 C. powdered sugar, sifted
½ C. finely chopped apricots
½ C. pecans, chopped

Combine first 5 ingredients with electric mixer until well blended. Gradually add 2 cups powdered sugar, mixing well with each addition. Knead in last cup of sugar, apricots and nutmeats with hands dusted with powdered sugar. Press into an 8" square pan. Cut in squares.

MEXICAN ORANGE

3 C. sugar
1½ C. rich milk, scalded
1/16 tsp. salt

Grated rind of 2 oranges
½ C. butter
1 C. broken black walnuts or
   pecan meats

Melt 1 cup sugar until smooth and deep golden color. Add scalded milk; stir thoroughly. Add remaining sugar and salt; stir until sugar dissolves and cook to soft ball stage (238°). Cool to lukewarm; add orange rind and butter. Beat until creamy; add nutmeats and pour on greased platter. Makes 30 pieces.

APPLETS

2 C. granulated sugar
¾ C. applesauce
2 T. unflavored gelatin

½ C. applesauce
2 tsp. vanilla
1 C. chopped nuts
Powdered sugar

Boil sugar and ¾ cup applesauce for 15 minutes. Add gelatin to remaining ½ cup applesauce; let stand 10 minutes before adding to cooked applesauce mixture. Add nuts and vanilla. Let stand at room temperature 24 hours in 7x11" pan. Cut into small oblong pieces. Sprinkle with powdered sugar. Place in sack with more powdered sugar and shake lightly.

CANDIED APPLES

6 wooden skewers
6 medium-size red apples
1 C. brown sugar
½ C. granulated sugar
½ C. light corn syrup

½ C. water
1 T. butter
1 tsp. vanilla extract
Finely chopped peanuts

Stick wooden skewers in stem end of apples. Cook sugars, corn syrup, water and butter in saucepan over low heat until sugar dissolves. Cook to light crack stage (272°) without stirring; remove from heat and add vanilla extract. Dip apples into syrup. Place upright on greased pan until cool or roll in finely chopped peanuts or other nutmeats. Makes 6 candied apples.

SNOW DROPS

8 dried apricot halves
1 C. water
2 C. sugar
⅛ tsp. salt

2 T. butter or fortified
  margarine
1 tsp. vanilla
1 C. shredded coconut

Cook apricots, covered, in water until soft. Add sugar, salt and butter. Cook to soft ball stage (234 to 236°). Add vanilla. Cool to lukewarm (110°). Beat until thick and creamy. Drop from a spoon into shredded coconut. Toss to cover with coconut. Cool on waxed paper. Makes 18 pieces. Soft ball test: Drop a small amount of mixture into cup of cold water. Mixture will form a ball that can be picked up in water, but will fall apart when taken out of water.

Under the "snow" there's creamy apricot candy.

FRUIT NUT BALLS

1 C. seedless raisins
1 C. pitted dates
1 C. pitted prunes
1 C. dried figs

1 C. California walnut
  meats
½ C. dried apricots
Melted semi-sweet
  chocolate

Mix together seedless raisins, pitted dates, pitted prunes, dried figs, California walnut meats and dried apricots, then place in food chopper, using coarse blade; mix well. Form in small balls. If desired, dip in melted chocolate; dry on cake rack covered with waxed paper. Makes 2½ dozen.

APRICOT SNOWBALLS

2 C. uncrushed cornflakes
  (or bran or wheat flakes)
⅓ C. diced, pitted dates
⅔ C. diced, dried California
  apricots
½ C. chopped pecans

¼ C. honey
3 T. butter or margarine
1 tsp. vanilla
Granulated sugar (optional)
Strips of dried California
  apricots, red glace cherry
  halves

Using a rolling pin, crush cornflakes between 2 sheets of waxed paper. Stir crushed cornflakes, dates, apricots and pecans until well mixed in large bowl. Melt honey and butter in small pan; blend in vanilla. Pour over cornflake mixture; mix thoroughly. Chill 30 minutes. Use 1 tablespoon of mixture to form each ball. Roll balls in sugar, if desired. Garnish each with a strip of apricot or a cherry half. Serve immediately or cover and chill until needed.

CHRISTMAS PATTIES

1 C. figs
1 C. dates
¼ C. seedless raisins
6 maraschino cherries

2 C. almonds
1 C. California walnuts
1 C. pecans
Sugar

Grind figs and dates, seedless raisins, maraschino cherries, almonds, California walnut meats and pecan meats; mix thoroughly. Form in small patties; dip in sugar. Keep in cool place. Makes about 3 dozen.

HARD CANDY

QUICK CARAMEL CORN

Popcorn   2 T. to ½ C. granulated
Shortening   sugar

You need a popper that can be stirred all the time to make this successfully.
Add your shortening and popcorn as usual to make regular popcorn. When
the corn fist starts to pop, add granulated sugar and stir until it is done
popping. Use more or less sugar according to the individual taste. The
popcorn will come out - coated with sugar.

BEST EVER PEANUT BRITTLE

3 C. sugar
1½ C. syrup
1⅓ C. water
Pinch of salt

2 C. raw peanuts
¼ C. butter or margarine
1 tsp. vanilla
1¼ tsp. water
1¼ tsp. soda

In heavy saucepan boil the sugar, syrup and water with a pinch of salt. Boil to 250°. Add the peanuts and butter; cook to 300°, stirring constantly. Remove from heat. Mix the vanilla, water and soda together and add to mixture. Stir the mixture (it will foam); after it settles down pour onto well oiled slab or good size cookie sheet. Spread out as best you can while pouring. Use buttered spoon or spatula to spread thin. Use spatula to loosen from bottom; turn over (you may need to cut in two to make it easier to handle). Using a pair of gloves, grab the edges of the brittle and stretch out as thin as possible. When cool, break in pieces and store in a cool airtight container.

POPCORN BALLS

⅓ C. light corn syrup
⅓ C. water
1 C. sugar
1 tsp. salt

¼ C. butter or margarine
1 tsp. vanilla
7 C. popped corn

Combine syrup, water, salt and butter in buttered 4-cup glass measure; cover. Microwave for 10 minutes on <u>defrost.</u> Stir and microwave for 5 minutes. Stir and microwave for 5 to 5½ minutes or until candy forms a hard ball (250°) in cold water. Stir in vanilla. Pour in thin stream over popped corn in large buttered bowl; mix well. Butter hands and shape into balls. Makes 10 to 12 balls.

TOFFEE

1 C. chopped, blanched
  almonds
1 C. butter

1 C. firmly packed brown
  sugar
2 bars sweet milk chocolate

Sprinkle ½ cup almonds over greased plate or pan. Melt butter; add sugar and mix thoroughly. Cook slowly, stirring constantly, to light crack stage (270°). Pour over almonds in thin sheet. When set, but still warm, arrange pieces of chocolate bars over mixture. As chocolate melts, spread over almonds with a spatula and sprinkle with remaining almonds. Cool and spread in pieces. Makes 1 dozen pieces.

PEANUT BRITTLE

1½ C. white sugar
1 C. white corn syrup
2 C. unroasted peanuts

Pinch of salt
1 T. butter
1 T. soda

Bring sugar, syrup, peanuts and salt to boil. Boil slowly 20 minutes. Then fast boil until brown, about 3 minutes. Stir in butter and soda. Mix well and pour into large, greased cookie sheet. It hardens immediately. Break up when cooled.

TRUFFLES

8 oz. dark sweet chocolate
  (Baker's German)
5 T. water
8 T. butter

3 T. light rum
Grated dark chocolate
Candy papers

Cut chocolate into small pieces and put in an ovenproof pan with water. Melt in oven to prevent burning. Cut butter into small pieces and add a little at a time to melted chocolate. Blend well. Stir in rum and cool in refrigerator for easier handling. Shape into ¾" balls and roll in grated chocolate. Place each ball in a candy paper.

CRACKER JACKS

½ C. butter or oleo
1½ C. brown sugar
½ C. water

1 C. white corn syrup
Pinch of salt
2½ qts. popped corn

Mix everything together, except popcorn and cook to hard ball, then remove from stove and pour over popcorn.

GORP

1 C. peanuts, lightly salted
1 C. raisins
1 C. coconut

1 C. sunflower seeds, lightly
 salted
1 C. each cereal - bran
 wheat and corn chex

Mix all ingredients together. Store in airtight container. Yields 20 servings, ⅓ cup each.

A FAVORITE PEANUT BRITTLE

2 C. sugar
1 C. light syrup
½ C. hot water
1 T. butter
1 tsp. baking soda

2 C. dry roasted salted
peanuts (You can
substitute other nuts or
coconut in place of
peanuts.)

Before you begin butter or oil a marble slab or 12x18" cookie sheet. Combine sugar, syrup and hot water in a 3-quart heavy saucepan. Stir with wooden spoon. Wash down sides with pastry brush dipped in water. Cook to 300°. Remove from heat, stir in butter, baking soda and nuts. Mix well. Mixture will be foamy. Pour out on slab and flatten with spoon and buttered spatula. Allow to cool for a few mintues. Then loosen from slab with spatula. Wearing gloves grasp candy by edges and stretch to thin it out. Let cool, then break in pieces.

WALNUT CHRISTMAS TOFFEE

1 C. butter (or part
  margarine)
1 C. granulated sugar
1 T. white corn syrup

3 T. water
1½ C. chopped walnuts
  (English)
1-6 oz. pkg. chocolate chips

Butter a 9" square pan. Melt butter in a 2-quart saucepan. Stir in sugar gradually. Add syrup and water; cook over moderate heat, stirring occasionally to 290° on candy thermometer or until a little mixture in cold water becomes very brittle. Add 1 cup walnuts. Cook 3 minutes more, stirring constantly. Pour into pan. When cold, remove from pan. Melt chocolate over hot water, coat one side of toffee. Sprinkle with chopped walnuts. Allow to sit a minute or so. Flip over on waxed paper and repeat. Break into bite-size pieces. Makes 1¾ pounds toffee.

MUNCHABLE BUTTER BRITTLE

1 C. pecans, chopped   ¾ C. brown sugar
½ C. butter   8 oz. chocolate chips

Spread chopped nuts in bottom of 9" square pan. Bring butter and sugar to boil. Boil 6 minutes. Pour over nuts. Spread chocolate chips over mixture until smooth.

CHOCOLATE WHISKEY BALLS

½ C. margarine, at room
  temperature
2 lbs. powdered sugar

1-15 oz. can sweetened
  condensed milk
2 T. whiskey
4 C. chopped pecans
Melted chocolate

Mix all ingredients together, except chocolate. Shape into 1" balls. Place in single layer on waxed paper. Let dry several hours or overnight. Reshape as needed and dip in melted chocolate (12 ounces of chocolate chips should do it). Place on wax paper. Let cool and harden.

KENTUCKY COLONELS

1 lb. powdered sugar
¼ lb. butter
1 T. evapoarted milk

Bourbon
1 lb. bittersweet chocolate
¼ block parawax
Pecans (halves)

Combine in mixing bowl sugar, butter and milk. Shape by hand this fondant into balls about size of small English walnut. With little finger shape a cavity into the ball. Be sure sides and bottom are not broken. With medicine dripper fill cavity with bourbon, do not fill too full. Pinch top together and use extra fondant if necessary to seal cavity. Melt chocolate and parawax. Dip balls in bittersweet chocolate using a dipping fork. Place on wax paper and place pecan half on top.

MICROWAVE PEANUT BRITTLE

1 C. raw peanuts
1 C. white sugar
½ C. white corn syrup
⅛ tsp. salt

1 T. margarine
1 tsp. soda
1 tsp. vanilla

Place peanuts, sugar, syrup and salt in 2-quart bowl. Cook 5 minutes on HIGH. Stir. Cook 2 more minutes. Add margarine and cook 1 to 1½ minutes. Add soda and vanilla and stir until fluffy. Pour onto buttered cookie sheet to cool.

CRISPY LOLLIPOPS

28 caramels
2 T. water
3 C. crispy rice cereal

1 C. raisins or chocolate
  chips
½ C. chopped, salted
  peanuts
12 wooden sticks

Melt caramels with water in double boiler over low heat. Stir until smooth. Pour over cereal, nuts and raisins or chocolate chips. Toss well with hands moistened with water and press into 9x9" pan. Cut and place sticks into 4½x1½" pieces. Wrap in plastic wrap.

ALMOND BUTTER CRUNCH

1 C. butter
1⅓ C. sugar
1 T. light corn syrup
3 T. water

1 C. **coarsely** chopped,
blanched almonds,
toasted
4-4½ oz. bars milk
chocolate, melted
1 C. **finely** chopped,
blanched almonds,
toasted

Melt butter in large saucepan. Add sugar, corn syrup and water. Cook, stirring occasionally, to hard crack stage (300°).* Quickly stir in coarsely chopped nuts; spread in ungreased 13x9½x2" pan. Cool thoroughly. Turn out on waxed paper; spread top with half the chocolate; sprinkle with <u>half</u> of finely chopped nuts. Cover with waxed paper; invert and spread again with chocolate. Sprinkle top with remaining nuts. If necessary, chill to firm chocolate. Break in pieces.

*Watch carefully after temperature reaches 280°.

It's a triple treat of chocolate, toffee and almonds.

LOLLIPOPS

3 C. sugar
¾ C. light corn syrup
3 tsp. vanilla
⅓ C. boiling water

¼ C. butter or margarine
Dash of salt
16 wooden skewers

Combine first 4 ingredients. Stir until sugar dissolves. Cook to hard crack stage (300°). Remove from heat; add butter and salt. Cool until slightly thick. Place sticks 5" apart on greased sheet. Drop candy from spoon over sticks to form 3" lollipops.

CANDY STICKS

2 C. sugar
½ C. water
½ C. light corn syrup

2 T. lemon juice
1½ T. lemon rind
1 tsp. flavoring
Food coloring

Combine sugar, water, corn syrup, lemon juice and lemon rind in a medium saucepan. Bring to a boil and continue boiling, without stirring, until mixture reaches crack stage (290°). Remove from heat and add flavoring and food coloring. Pour onto a buttered platter. When candy is cool enough to handle, pull and twist into canes or sticks.

Try peppermint extract with red food coloring, lemon with yellow and cinnamon with red or brown. (To color candy brown, combine red and yellow food coloring with a drop of blue.)

BUTTERSCOTCH LOLLIPOPS

3 C. sugar
¾ C. light corn syrup
3 T. vinegar
⅓ C. boiling water

¼ C. butter
Dash of salt
½ tsp. yellow food coloring
Wooden skewers

Combine sugar, corn syrup, vinegar and water; stir until sugar dissolves. Cook to hard crack stage (300°). Remove from heat; add butter, salt and coloring. Drop from tablespoon over skewers on greased cookie sheet to form lollipops. Makes 4 dozen.

CANDY WITH NUTS

WALNUT CANDY

2 C. sugar
½ C. water
⅛ tsp. salt
2 T. light syrup

⅔ T. mint extract
4 rounded T. marshmallow
 creme
6 C. large walnuts

Cook sugar, water, salt and corn syrup to soft ball stage (235°). Add mint and marshmallow creme. When melted into mixture, remove from heat and add nuts. Working quickly fold nuts until all are coated. Pour out on large cookie sheet and spread with spoon or spatula. When cool enough to handle, separate nuts.

PRALINES

2 C. sugar
1 C. packed brown sugar
½ C. milk
1-6 oz. can evaporated
 milk

¼ C. butter or margarine
¼ tsp. salt
3 C. coarsely chopped
 pecans

Combine all ingredients except nuts in buttered large glass mixing bowl; cover. Microwave on <u>defrost</u> for 20 minutes. Stir and microwave for 15 to 20 minutes or until a soft ball forms in cold water. Beat with mixer at medium speed until creamy. Stir in nuts. Pour in 9x13" dish. Cool until firm. Cut in pieces.

CANDY-COATED NUTMEATS

1 C. brown sugar
½ C. granulated sugar
½ C. sour cream

1 tsp. vanilla extract
2½ C. California walnut
  halves or pecans

Combine brown sugar, granulated sugar and sour cream; cook to soft ball stage (236°). Add vanilla extract; beat until it begins to thicken. Add California walnut halves or pecans; stir until well coated. Turn out on greased platter or cookie sheet; separate in individual pieces. Makes 2 dozen pieces.

YUMMY WALNUTS

1 C. brown sugar
½ C. granulated sugar
2 T. light corn syrup
¼ C. milk

1 T. margarine
1 tsp. vanilla extract
1½ C. California walnut
  meats

Combine brown sugar, granulated sugar, light corn syrup and milk. Cook to soft ball stage (236°). Add margarine and vanilla extract; beat until creamy. Add California walnut meats; stir until well coated. Turn into greased pan; separate into individual pieces. Makes about 2 dozen.

PRALINES

1 C. sugar
½ C. heavy cream
3 T. dark corn syrup
1/16 tsp. baking soda

1/16 tsp. salt
1 C. pecan halves
½ tsp. vanilla

In heavy 2-quart saucepan, stir together sugar, cream, syrup, baking soda and salt. Cook over medium heat, stirring occasionally, until sugar dissolves and mixture comes to a boil. Continue baking until mixture reaches 230° on candy thermometer or until soft ball ball flattens on removal from water. Remove from heat, add pecans and vanilla, stirring until creamy and mixture covers pecans with s slight opaque coating. Drop by heaping teaspoon onto waxed paper. Cool and store between layers of waxed paper in covered tin box.

CHOCOLATE COVERED NUTS

½ stick butter
6 oz. unsweetened
   chocolate
2 T. liquid sweetener

½ tsp. vanilla
8 oz. nut halves

Melt butter and chocolate over low heat. Add other ingredients, except nuts. Remove from heat and add nuts. Drop in clusters on waxed paper.

CARAMEL NUT ROLLS

1-7½ oz. jar marshmallow
  creme
1 tsp. vanilla

3½ C. powdered sugar
1 lb. caramels
9½ C. chopped nuts

Combine marshmallow creme and vanilla; add sugar gradually. Shape into rolls about 1" in diameter. Wrap in plastic wrap and freeze for at least 6 hours. Melt caramels over hot water; keep warm. Dip candy rolls in caramels, then roll in nuts until well coated. Store cooled candy in a covered container. Makes about 5 pounds.

PECAN SPICE CANDY

⅔ C. honey
2 C. non-instant dry
  powdered milk
3 tsp. cinnamon
8 T. water

½ C. pecan pieces
2 tsp. allspice
2 tsp. carob powder
2 tsp. vanilla

Mix all the ingredients together. Use the milk as a dry powder. Beat until smooth. Butter a 10x6" glass dish and press in candy. Cut into small pieces. Refrigerate. Then, enjoy.

APRICOT ACORNS

1-8 oz. can almond paste,
  crumbled
½ C. wheat germ
1 C. honey

½ C. sesame seeds
2 C. instant nonfat dry milk
36 dried apricots
  (about 8 oz.)
36 whole cloves

In a bowl, mix almond paste, wheat germ, honey, sesame seeds and milk powder until the mixture is smooth and thoroughly combined. Shape into 36 balls. Place apricot half on one side of each ball. Fasten apricot in place with a whole clove. Pinch the other side of the ball into a point to resemble an acorn. Place acorns side by side in a single layer on waxed paper or foil and let dry at room temperature. Store in an airtight container in a cool, dry place until ready to serve.

SWEDISH NUTS

2 egg whites
1 C. sugar

1 lb. pecans
¼ lb. butter, melted

Beat egg whites until stiff and add sugar. Beat well together. Toast pecans (15 minutes at 300°). Put melted butter in baking pan and add nuts and egg whites. Blend. Bake 45 minutes, stirring every 15 minutes until golden brown.

CHOCOLATE PEANUT CLUSTERS

2 C. white sugar
1 C. evaporated milk
24 caramels

1½ C. chocolate chips
1 tsp. vanilla
1 lb. salted peanuts

Mix and dissolve white sugar and evaporated milk on medium heat. Add caramels. Bring to boil and boil 4 minutes. Take from heat and add chips, vanilla and peanuts. Stir and drop on waxed paper.

PECAN ROLL

3 C. white sugar
¼ C. white corn syrup

⅛ tsp. soda
1 C. cream, sweet or sour

Boil all ingredients to a little over soft ball stage, about 240°. Cook, stir and cream up like chocolate drop centers. Work with hands and shape in rolls.

CARAMEL PART:
1½ C. white sugar
¼ lb. butter
¾ C. white corn syrup

½ tsp. vanilla
1 C. sweet cream
2½ C. pecan halves

Cook sugar, butter, and syrup slowly, stirring occasionally. Cook to 240°. Remove from heat, add vanilla and sweet cream. Dip rolls in hot caramel, then roll in pecan halves. Press nuts into caramel with hands. Cool. Wrap in Saran Wrap. When cool, slice in 1" pieces.

CANDY COATED NUTS

1 C. brown sugar
½ C. white sugar
½ C. sour cream

1 tsp. vanilla
2½ C. nutmeats

Cook brown sugar, white sugar, and sour cream to soft ball stage (236°).
Add flavoring and beat until mixture begins to thicken. Then add nutmeats.
Stir until well coated. Pour on waxed paper. Separate as soon as nuts are
cool enough to handle.

PECAN PRALINES

1½ C. sugar
1 C. dark brown sugar
 (do not pack)
½ tsp. salt

½ C. evaporated milk
½ stick butter or oleo
2 tsp. vanilla
2 C. whole pecans

Cook sugar, salt and milk in a heavy saucepan over medium heat, until it comes to a rolling boil (do not stir). Add butter and stir until it has melted. Remove pan from fire; add vanilla, nuts and mix well. Stir until it thickens. Drop by spoonfuls onto wax paper. Let candy cool and remove carefully from wax paper. Makes 2 dozen.

PECAN TASSIES

2 sticks butter   3 oz. cream cheese
2 C. flour

FILLING:
2 eggs   2 tsp. melted butter
½ tsp. salt   1 tsp. vanilla
1½ C. brown sugar   Chopped pecans

Blend butter and Philadelphia cream cheese. Add 2 cups of flour (½ cup at a time). Mix and press into small muffin tins.

FILLING: <u>DO NOT COOK</u>. Combine (in order) eggs, salt, brown sugar, melted butter and vanilla.

Put chopped pecans in muffin tins and put in filling. Top with chopped pecans. Bake at 350° for 5 to 7 minutes. Then turn to 250° until set, about 10 minutes. These freeze beautifully. Can be prepared ahead of time for the holidays or whatever reason.

TURTLES

2 C. light cream
1½ C. white sugar
½ tsp. salt
½ C. brown sugar

1 C. light corn syrup
⅓ C. butter
1 tsp. vanilla
Pecans, as desired
Melted chocolate

In heavy saucepan, heat cream to lukewarm. Pour out 1 cup and reserve. To remaining cream in saucepan, add sugar, corn syrup and salt. Cook over moderate heat and stir until it boils. Very slowly stir in reserved cream (1 cup) so mixture does not stop boiling. Cook and stir constantly for 5 minutes. Stir in butter, about 1 teaspoon at a time. Turn heat low. Boil gently and stir part time until temperature reaches 248°, or until small amount dropped in cold water forms a firm ball that does not flatten when removed from water. Remove from heat. Gently stir in vanilla and cool slightly. Pour over pecans placed in a cake pan. When cold, cut in squares and dip in chocolate.

CARAMEL NUTS

1 C. brown sugar
½ C. granulated sugar
½ C. light cream
2 T. corn syrup

1 T. butter or margarine
1 T. vanilla
2 C. California walnut halves

Combine sugars, cream and corn syrup; cook to soft ball stage (236°). Add butter and vanilla. Cool at room temperature, without stirring, until lukewarm (110°). Beat until mixture begins to lose gloss; add nuts and stir until well coated. Turn out on waxed paper; separate nuts with 2 forks. Makes about 4 cups.

WALNUT KISSES

1 C. white sugar
1 C. brown sugar
½ C. evaporated milk
2 T. margarine

¼ tsp. salt
1 tsp. vanilla
1½ C. walnuts (English)

Cook sugar, milk, and margarine over medium heat, stir occasionally, until mixture forms soft ball. Add salt and vanilla. Cook 1 more minute and add English walnuts. Beat until thick. Drop on waxed paper.

BUTTERMILK CANDY

2 C. sugar
1 C. buttermilk
¼ C. butter
½ tsp. soda

2 T. syrup
A lot of pecans
1 tsp. vanilla

Mix everything together, except vanilla, and cook over medium heat until it boils and thickens. Set off heat and add vanilla. When lukewarm, beat until thick as for fudge. Pour out into buttered plate. This candy turns a rich brown before your eyes!

HEAVENLY HASH

2 C. marshmallows
3 C. sugar
1½ C. evaporated milk
½ C. cocoa

¼ C. butter or margarine
2 C. chopped pecans
1¾ C. marshmallow creme
1 tsp. vanilla

Cut marshmallows in pieces and place in a greased 9x12" pan. Mix sugar, milk, cocoa and butter. Cook mixture until a soft ball is formed when dropped into water (235°). Add pecans, marshmallow creme and vanilla. Beat until mixture begins to thicken. Pour over the broken pieces of marshmallows. Let cool before cutting.

BUTTERSCOTCH PUDDING CANDY

1 pkg. butterscotch pudding
 (not instant)
1 C. white sugar

½ C. milk
1 T. butter
½ C. brown sugar
1½ C. pecans

Boil all ingredients, <u>except pecans</u> until it reaches soft ball test in cold water (boil about 3 minutes). Remove from stove, add pecans and beat a short time. Drop by tablespoons on waxed paper.

DATE ROLL CANDY

2 C. sugar
½ C. light syrup
½ C. water
Dash of salt

Dash of cream of tartar
2-10 oz. pkgs. pitted dates,
  chopped coarsely
1 C. pecans, chopped

Mix together all ingredients except dates and nuts. Bring to rolling boil. Add dates and cook to soft ball stage (235°). Remove from stove and beat until mixture becomes very thick. Add nutmeats and mix. Pour onto damp towel and roll. Place in refrigerator.

CHURCH WINDOWS

½ C. margarine
1-12 oz. pkg. chocolate
  chips

1-10½ oz. pkg. colored
  miniature marshmallows
1 C. chopped walnuts
1 C. flaked coconut

In top of double boiler, melt together margarine and chocolate chips. Place marshmallows and nuts in large bowl. Pour chocolate mixture over marshmallows and nuts; blending carefully. Sprinkle ⅓ cup coconut on a piece of wax paper and pour one-third of marshmallow mixture on paper. Roll the paper into an oblong or tube shape. Repeat for 2 more rolls. Refrigerate for 1 hour. Remove wax paper from rolls and slice each roll into about 12 pieces.

HONEY NUT CANDY

3 T. butter
½ C. honey

Nonfat dry milk
½ C. ground nuts

Melt butter. Add honey. Mix in enough nonfat dry milk to make a thick mixture. Add ground nuts. Form into a roll and chill. Slice and enjoy!

SOFT CANDY

CHRISTMAS CANDY

White chocolate or almond bark

Salted pretzels
Salted peanuts

Melt white chocolate or almond bark in double boiler. Mix in broken salted pretzels and salted peanuts. Spread quickly on waxed paper or buttered cookie sheet. Cool, break into bite-sized pieces

DANDY DIVINITY

2 C. sugar
⅔ C. light corn syrup
½ C. water

2 stiffly-beaten egg whites
1 tsp. vanilla
1 C. walnuts, if desired

Combine sugar, corn syrup and water. Stir over low heat until sugar dissolves. Cook over medium heat until light crack stage, 270°. Slowly pour over egg whites, beating constantly, with beater. Add vanilla. Beat until mixture holds shape. Drop from teaspoon onto wax paper.

DIVINITY FUDGE

3 C. sugar
½ C. light syrup
½ C. cold water

2 egg whites
1 tsp. vanilla
Nutmeats (optional)

Place sugar, syrup and water in pan over low heat. Stir only until sugar is dissolved, then cook until a little tried in cold water forms a soft ball. Beat egg whites until stiff, continue beating and pouring ½ the syrup mixture slowly over the beaten egg whites, beating all the time, continue beating. Meanwhile, cook the remaining ½ of the syrup mixture until it forms a hard ball when tried in cold water and cracks when it hits the side of the cup. Now add this syrup gradually to the egg mixture, beating all the time. Add vanilla and beat until mixture is thick enough to pour in pans. If nutmeats are added, mix in with a spoon and pour in pans.

PEANUT BUTTER BALLS

1 C. margarine
2 C. peanut butter
3 C. powdered sugar

1½ tsp. vanilla
3 C. crispy rice cereal or
   cocoa crispy rice cereal
½ bar paraffin
1-8 oz. pkg. chocolate chips

Melt margarine and stir in next 4 ingredients. Roll into small balls. Melt ½ bar of paraffin and 1-8 ounce package of chocolate chips. Dip ball in chocolate mixture and turn. Cool on a cookie sheet or wax paper.

TAFFY

4 C. white sugar
2 C. sweet cream
2 C. light corn syrup

Parawax, size of a walnut
1 pkg. Knox gelatin
Food coloring

Mix altogether and cook to 250°, stirring occasionally. Pour in greased pans and set in a cold place. Pull as soon as cold enough to handle. The harder and faster this is pulled, the lighter it gets. When almost done, pull in ropes and twist. Grease hands lightly when pulling, but too much grease (butter) will make your taffy "part". A few drops of coloring added while pulling makes a nice effect. Cut in bite-size pieces when almost cold. You may wrap each piece separately. Let age for a month or more and it will get mellow.

CHOCOLATE NUT CREAMS

½ C. sugar
Pinch of salt
½ C. enriched flour
2 T. margarine
2 egg yolks

1 C. milk
1-6 oz. pkg. semi-sweet
  chocolate chips
1 C. finely chopped
  California walnuts

Mix sugar, salt and enriched flour. Add margarine, egg yolks, milk. Cook in double boiler, stirring constantly, until thick enough to hold shape. Gradually add semi-sweet chocolate chips; stir until melted. Chill. Drop from teaspoon into finely chopped California walnut meats. Form balls. Chill. Makes 2 dozen.

OATMEAL SQUARES

1 C. flaked coconut
3 C. rolled oats
½ C. chopped pecans
½ tsp. salt

½ C. cocoa
2 C. sugar
½ C. milk
½ C. butter
1 tsp. vanilla

Combine coconut, oats, pecans and salt in large mixing bowl. Place cocoa, sugar, milk, butter and vanilla in a saucepan; heat to boiling point. Boil for 2 minutes. Pour over oatmeal mixture; blend well. Spread in foil-lined 11x7x1½" pan. Refrigerate. Cut into small squares. Makes about 5 dozen.

YUMMY PEANUT BARS

½ lb. semi-sweet chocolate
  chips
¼ tsp. salt

⅔ C. raisins or dates,
  chopped fine
⅔ C. chopped peanuts
⅓ C. chopped peanuts for
  the top

Melt chips in double boiler or microwave until smooth. Then add salt, raisins, peanuts and mix well. Spread in a buttered, shallow pan to ¼" depth. Sprinkle ⅓ cup nuts over the top. When set, cut into strips.

SEAFOAM

2½ C. white sugar
½ C. dark corn syrup
½ C. water

2 egg whites
½ C. chopped nuts

Boil sugar, syrup and water until mixture reaches hard crack stage. Beat the egg whites until very stiff. Pour hot syrup slowly over egg whites with the mixer running at high speed. Then beat until stiff enough to drop. Add nuts and drop onto wax paper. Work quickly as mixture thickens rapidly.

MARZIPAN

8 oz. almond paste
¼ C. corn syrup

¾ C. marshmallow creme
1 lb. powdered sugar

Combine ingredients; blend with hands. Form into fruit shapes. Paint with food coloring dissolved in water.

MARSHMALLOW NUT PUFFS

Marshmallows
Cream
Vanilla

Pecan meats, ground
Shredded coconut
Chocolate decorates

Dip marshmallows in hot cream, flavored with vanilla, until outside of marshmallows are soft. Roll in finely ground pecan meats, moist shredded coconut, or chocolate decorates; flatten slightly. Chill.

TOLL HOUSE MARBLE SQUARES

½ C. butter, softened
6 T. granulated sugar
½ tsp. vanilla
¼ tsp. water
6 T. brown sugar
1 egg

1 C. plus 2 T. flour
½ tsp. soda
½ tsp. salt
½ C. chopped nuts
6 oz. (1 C.) chocolate chips

Blend softened butter, granulated sugar, vanilla, water, brown sugar. Beat in egg. Add and mix well flour, soda, salt. Stir in chopped nuts. Spread in greased baking dish, then sprinkle chocolate chips over batter. Place in 375° oven for 1 minute. Remove from oven and run knife through batter to marbleize it. Return to oven and bake at 375° for 10 to 12 minutes.

CHOCOLATE BUTTERSCOTCH TREAT

1 pkg. chocolate chips
1 pkg. butterscotch chips

1 C. peanuts
1 can chow mein noodles

Melt chocolate chips and butterscotch chips. Mix into the liquid, peanuts and chow mein noodles. Drop by spoonful onto waxed paper. No refrigeration is needed.

SALTED NUT BARS

1-12 oz. pkg. peanut butter
  chips
1 can sweetened condensed
  milk

2 C. miniature
  marshmallows
1 tsp. vanilla
Chopped dry roasted
  peanuts

Melt peanut butter chips, sweetened condensed milk, marshmallows and vanilla over low heat. Refrigerate until cool. Form into mini-logs and roll in chopped dry roasted peanuts.

MARVELOUS MARSHMALLOWS

1 chocolate bar   Chopped nuts
Marshmallows

Melt a chocolate bar in the top of double boiler. Stick a toothpick in a marshmallow. Dip in chocolate and roll in chopped nuts.

SWEET NOTHINGS

2 sticks margarine
1 C. peanut butter
2 C. chocolate chips

1 tsp. vanilla
1-12 oz. box rice chex cereal
4 C. powdered sugar

Melt the margarine, peanut butter, chocolate chips, and vanilla together in a double boiler just until melted; stirring constantly. Pour over 1-12 ounce box rice chex. Coat with 4 cups sifted powdered sugar.

ORANGE-BUTTER FONDANT

3 C. powdered sugar
3 T. butter

6 T. orange juice
Pitted dates or prunes
Thin slices of candied
  orange peel, walnuts,
  or pecan halves

Cream powdered sugar with butter; add orange juice to moisten. Fill pitted dates or prunes, topping each with a thin slice of candied orange peel or a walnut or pecan half.

CREOLE PRALINES

3 C. sugar
1 C. water
1 tsp. vinegar

1 T. margarine
3 C. pecan meats

Combine sugar, water and vinegar. Cook to soft ball stage (236°). Add margarine and nutmeats; remove from heat. Beat until mixture starts to thicken. Drop from teaspoon onto waxed paper. Cool. Makes 3 dozen pralines.

PEPPERMINT PRALINES: Add ½ teaspoon peppermint extract.

FONDANT - STUFFED DATES

4½ C. powdered sugar
⅔ C. sweetened condensed
  milk
1 tsp. vanilla

1 tsp. almond extract
4 doz. pitted dates
Granulated or powdered
  sugar

Blend powdered sugar, milk, vanilla and almond extract. Knead fondant until smooth and creamy. Wrap in foil or plastic wrap and refrigerate 24 hours. Fill each date with fondant; roll in sugar. Yield: about 4 dozen candies.

SKILLET CANDIES

1 C. melted butter
1½ C. light brown sugar
2 C. cut-up dates
2 T. milk
½ tsp. salt

2 eggs, beaten
1 C. chopped nuts
1 tsp. vanilla
4 C. crispy rice cereal
Coconut

Melt butter; add sugar and dates. Cook over low heat. Add milk and salt and slowly stir in beaten eggs. Bring to a boil and boil for 3 minutes. Remove from heat. When cool, add nuts, vanilla and cereal. Stir to mix well. Use a teaspoon to form candy into balls. Roll in coconut. Makes about 6 dozen.

DOT'S MINTS

¼ C. margarine
1 lb. powdered sugar
½ egg white

½ tsp. oil of peppermint
2 drops food coloring
Very little bit of cream

Mix all ingredients well. Amount of cream to use depends on consistency of mixture (should be about as thick as softened butter). Form into small pattles or force thru star-shape cookie press. Place on wax paper and let sit for 12 hours. Store in container.

HOLIDAY MINTS

3 egg whites
6 C. powdered sugar
Red and green food coloring

½ tsp. peppermint extract
½ tsp. spearmint extract

Beat egg whites until stiff, adding sugar gradually. Divide candy into 2 portions. Tint half green and half red. Add peppermint extract to red mixture and spearmint extract to green mixture. Roll candy between 2 pieces of waxed paper. Cut with small round cookie cutter. Let dry overnight.

TOASTED ALMOND BALLS

1 C. semi-sweet chocolate
  chips
1 C. butterscotch chips
¾ C. powdered sugar
½ C. cultured sour cream

1½ tsp. grated orange rind
¼ tsp. salt
2 C. vanilla wafer crumbs
¾ C. finely chopped, toasted
  almonds

Melt chocolate and butterscotch chips at a low heat. Mix in sugar, sour cream, orange rind, salt and crumbs; chill. Shape into ¾" balls; roll in almonds. Makes about 6½ dozen.

BOURBON BALLS

1 C. vanilla wafer crumbs
1 C. finely chopped pecans
1 C. powdered sugar
2 T. cocoa

¼ C. bourbon
1½ T. light corn syrup
Confectioners' sugar for
  rolling

Mix crumbs, pecans, sugar and cocoa. Blend bourbon and syrup. Combine mixtures. Shape into balls; roll in sugar. Refrigerate.

RUM BALLS

2 C. fine graham cracker
  crumbs
½ C. finely chopped nuts

¼ C. melted butter
¼ C. rum
¼ to ½ lb. chocolate bark

Mix first 4 ingredients well. Shape into small balls. Refrigerate while melting chocolate. Dip balls into melted chocolate. Place on waxed paper and refrigerate until set.

PEANUT BUTTER BALLS

1 lb. powdered sugar
1 stick margarine
3 C. crispy rice cereal
2 C. peanut butter

COATING:
12 oz. chocolate chips
½ bar paraffin
(Melt together in double
  boiler, mixing well.)

Mix together first 4 ingredients and make into 1½" balls. Dip in melted coating mixture. Makes 70 to 75 balls.

WHITE TAFFY

1 C. sugar
⅓ C. water
4 T. light corn syrup

1 T. vinegar
¼ tsp. soda

Combine sugar, water and corn syrup; stir over low heat until sugar dissolves. Cook, without stirring, to light crack stage (270°). Remove from heat; add vinegar and soda and mix thoroughly. Pour on greased platter to cool. Pull until taffy is snow-white and porous. If necessary, fat may be used on hands to prevent sticking. When candy is too hard to pull, twist in rope of desired thickness. Cool and break in pieces about 1½" long. Makes 2 dozen pieces.

BUCKEYES

These candies look like the real thing and are sure to cause comment.

*1-18 oz. jar creamy peanut
  butter, room temperature
½ lb. butter or margarine,
  softened*

*1½ lbs. powdered sugar
1-12 oz. pkg. chocolate
  chips*

Mix peanut butter, butter and sugar together until smooth texture. Form into small balls the size of buckeyes. Refrigerate 2 or 3 hours. Melt chocolate in double boiler. Using a toothpick, dip the cold buckeyes into chocolate, leave about ⅓ uncovered. Dry on wax paper.

BUTTERSCOTCH SURPRISE

2-6 oz. pkgs. butterscotch
  chips
½ C. peanut butter

1 C. nuts
1 to 1½ oz. can shoestring
  potatoes

Melt butterscotch chips and peanut butter in top of double boiler. Stir in
nuts and shoestring potatoes. Drop on waxed paper. Cool in refrigerator.

CHOCOLATE COVERED CANDY

2 lbs. powdered sugar
1 lb. butter
1 can condensed milk

Finely chopped pecans
 and/or cherries
Melted chocolate for dipping

Mix sugar, butter and condensed milk. Roll into balls the size of small walnuts. Roll in chopped nuts or work ball around cherries or both. Freeze hard. Then dip frozen candy balls into chocolate.

CARAMEL SNAPPERS

144 small pecan halves
36 light caramels

½ C. semi-sweet chocolate
chips, melted

Arrange pecan halves (flat side down) in groups of 4 on slightly-buttered baking sheet. Place one caramel on each cluster. Heat in slow oven (325°) until caramel softens (4 to 8 minutes). Remove from oven. Flatten caramel with buttered spatula. Cool slightly and remove from pan to waxed paper. Swirl chocolate on top. Let harden.

CARAMELS

2 C. sugar
1½ C. white syrup
3 C. whipping cream

4 T. butter
2 tsp. vanilla
Nuts (optional)

Cook sugar, syrup and 1 cup cream over low heat, stirring constantly, until mixture reaches 238°. Add 1 more cup cream slowly so mixture doesn't stop boiling and it reaches 238° again. Add last cup of cream in same manner and boil to 248°. Remove from fire and add butter and vanilla. Pour into buttered pan. Add nuts, if desired.

For chocolate caramels, add 3 tablespoons cocoa to sugar, syrup and cream.

NO COOK CANDY

1 pkg. cream cheese,
  softened
1 pkg. flaked coconut

1-2 oz. pkg. lemon flavored
  gelatin
1 T. sugar
1 C. finely chopped nuts

In large bowl, thoroughly combine first 4 ingredients. Chill until firm. Roll in 1" balls. Coat balls with nuts. Chill. Cover tightly and store in refrigerator. Makes about 3 dozen.

MOUNDS CANDY

1 stick margarine
1 can sweetened condensed
  milk
Pinch of salt

2 lbs. powdered sugar
1 can coconut
12 oz. pkg. chocolate chips
1/3 cake paraffin

Melt margarine, add salt and milk. Mix in 2 pounds powdered sugar. Mix well. Add coconut. Roll into balls and freeze overnight. Dip balls into 12 ounce package of chocolate chips and paraffin which have been melted together. Place on waxed paper and cool.

CANDY PUFFS

1 C. corn syrup
2½ C. brown sugar
½ C. water

1 tsp. vinegar
1 T. butter
18 oz. pkg. puffed wheat cereal

Cook all together syrup, brown sugar, water, and vinegar until syrup forms a soft ball when tried in cold water. Add 1 tablespoon butter and stir until it is all melted. Pour over puffed wheat cereal in buttered pan and mix well. Press in buttered cake pan and cut when cool.

Variation: Instead of puffed wheat, other cereals may be used, one alone or mixed and nutmeats added.

PEANUT BUTTER CANDY

1 well-beaten egg
⅛ tsp. salt
½ tsp. vanilla
1 T. butter

⅓ C. peanut butter
2 C. powdered sugar
¾ C. chopped, salted nuts

Mix egg, salt, vanilla, butter and peanut butter with 1 cup of powdered sugar. Beat together well, then stir in the second cup of sugar. Add more powdered sugar, if needed, to make firm enough to handle. Shape into tiny balls. Roll each ball in chopped, salted nuts. Place on waxed paper and refrigerate to set.

MARZIPAN

4 T. butter
4 T. light corn syrup
¼ tsp. salt
¼ tsp. almond extract

½ tsp. vanilla
2 C. powdered sugar
  substitute
8 oz. almond paste
1 C. nonfat dry milk

Cream butter, gradually adding syrup, salt, almond extract and vanilla. Alternately add sugar substitute and almond paste. Finally, add powdered milk. It should be the consistency of pie dough. Form into fruit shapes. Paint with food coloring, dissolved in water. Enjoy!

GREEN WREATHS

32 large marshmallows
6 T. butter
½ tsp. vanilla
½ tsp. almond extract

1 tsp. green food coloring
4 C. cornflakes
Red cinnamon candies

Melt marshmallows and butter in large saucepan over low heat. Mix in flavorings and food coloring. Add cornflakes and stir until coated. Place pan over hot water; stir occasionally. Butter hands well. Drop mixture from spoon onto waxed paper; form into wreaths immediately. Decorate with cinnamon candies before wreaths harden. Makes 2 dozen or more, depending on size.

SEAFOAM CANDY

3 C. sugar
½ C. light corn syrup
⅔ C. water
2 egg whites

⅛ tsp. salt
1 tsp. vanilla
1 C. nuts (optional)

Boil sugar, syrup and water until it forms a hard ball when dropped in water. Beat egg whites and salt for 3 minutes with mixer on high. Slowly pour syrup into egg whites, beating with mixer until mixture passes glossy stage. Add nuts and vanilla and beat until a peak forms when beater is raised. Pour into an 8x8" pan or drop on waxed paper.

TURKISH DELIGHTS

1 C. applesauce
1-6 oz. or 2-3 oz. pkgs.
  flavored gelatin

1 C. granulated sugar
⅔ C. chopped nuts

Heat applesauce and dissolve gelatin in sauce. Add sugar and boil 1 minute. Add nuts. Pour in 8" square pan. Chill. Cut and roll in sugar. After 24 hours, roll in sugar again.

ROCKY ROAD CANDY

2 lbs. milk chocolate
½ lb. soft butter

10 oz. miniature
  marshmallows
3 lbs. nuts (broken)

Melt chocolate, stir until smooth. Add butter and mix well. (Will be thick, but warm.) Set in cold place until it thickens around edges (stir occasionally while cooling). Bring into warm room and stir 5 to 10 minutes until creamy and thinner. Add marshmallows and nuts. Pour into greased cookie sheet. Press ¾" thick and cool. Cut in squares at room temperature.

PEANUT BUTTER CUPS

⅓ C. creamy peanut butter
¼ C. sifted powdered sugar

1 tsp. vanilla
8 oz. chocolate almond bark

Blend peanut butter, powdered sugar and vanilla and chill. Shape by using ½ teaspoon and roll into balls. Place in 1½" paper bonbon cups fitted into miniature muffin pans. Melt chocolate almond bark. Spoon over balls of filling cups. Chill.

CHOW MEIN NOODLE CANDY

2 pkgs. chocolate chips
2 pkgs. butterscotch chips

1 large can chow mein
  noodles
1 lb. cashew nuts

Melt chips in double boiler. Add chow mein noodles and cashew nuts. Mix well and drop on wax paper.

FRUIT CRUNCH

2 lbs. white almond bark
11 oz. fruit loops cereal
  (may use only 10 oz.)
1 lb. chopped dates

1½ C. chopped nuts
1 pkg. miniature colored
  marshmallows

Melt bark in double boiler. Pour over other mixed ingredients or stir in lightly so breakfast food doesn't break into crumbs. Spoon onto wax paper. Break into small pieces after it has cooled.